Finding Light

Finding Light

Edith Cosgrove

CONTENTS

Understanding Seasonal Affective Disord

The Science Behind SAD

Seasonal Affective Disorder (SAD) is a type of depression that typically occurs during the fall and winter months when daylight hours are shorter. The onset of SAD is closely linked to changes in light exposure, which can significantly affect our mood and behavior. The reduced availability of natural sunlight can lead to imbalances in our internal biological clock, or circadian rhythm, disrupting our sleep patterns, energy levels, and overall emotional well-being. Understanding the science behind SAD helps to demystify the experiences of those affected and sheds light on potential coping mechanisms.

At the heart of SAD is the role of serotonin, a neurotransmitter that influences mood, appetite, and sleep. Sunlight exposure is crucial for the production of serotonin, and during darker months, levels can drop significantly. This decline can lead to feelings of sadness, lethargy, and a general disinterest in daily activities. Many individuals with SAD report a craving for carbohydrates, which can further exacerbate weight gain and feelings of low self-worth, creating a cycle that is difficult to break. Recognizing the biochemical underpinnings of these feelings can foster greater compassion towards oneself during difficult times.

Melatonin, another hormone affected by light exposure, plays a significant role in regulating sleep patterns. As daylight wanes, melatonin production increases, often leading to excessive sleepiness and disrupted sleep-wake cycles. The interplay between serotonin and melatonin during the holiday season can be particularly challenging. With holiday festivities often extending late into the evening, maintaining a regular sleep schedule becomes increasingly difficult. This disruption not only affects mood but can also hinder the ability to engage in mindfulness practices that promote relaxation and stress relief.

Mindfulness techniques can be invaluable in managing the symptoms of SAD, especially during the hectic holiday season. Practices such as meditation, deep breathing, and gentle yoga can help ground individuals, fostering a sense of calm amidst the chaos. These techniques encourage a greater awareness of one's thoughts and feelings, enabling individuals to navigate the emotional landscape of the holidays with more ease. Incorporating even short bursts of mindfulness throughout the day can make a significant difference in coping with stress and maintaining emotional balance.

Creating a stress-free holiday calendar that respects personal boundaries is essential for those managing SAD. Prioritizing self-care routines, such as scheduled downtime and engaging in activities that bring joy, can enhance resilience against the seasonal gloom. Communicating openly with family members about one's needs during this time fosters understanding and support. By approaching the holiday season with a focus on well-being and connection, individuals can illuminate their path through the darkness, finding light in moments of joy and togetherness.

Recognizing Symptoms and Triggers

Recognizing the symptoms and triggers of Seasonal Affective Disorder (SAD) is a crucial step in managing the emotional challenges that often accompany the holiday season. Many individuals may experience a range of symptoms during this time, including persistent feelings of sadness, fatigue, irritability, or changes in sleep and appetite. It is essential to acknowledge that these feelings are not merely a result of holiday stress but can be exacerbated by the reduced sunlight and shorter days typical of winter. By understanding these symptoms, individuals can take proactive steps to seek support and develop coping strategies tailored to their unique circumstances.

Holiday gatherings, while often filled with joy, can also be significant triggers for those suffering from SAD. The expectations surrounding family dynamics during this time can create pressure that intensifies feelings of inadequacy or sadness. Recognizing the specific situations that lead to heightened anxiety or distress is vital. Whether it's the pressure to maintain family traditions, navigate complex relationships, or the sheer busyness of the season, being aware of these triggers can empower individuals to set boundaries and prioritize their mental health.

Mindfulness techniques can serve as powerful tools for managing both SAD and holiday stress. Practicing mindfulness involves being present in the moment and acknowledging one's feelings without judgment. Simple exercises, such as deep breathing or guided imagery, can help ground individuals during moments of overwhelm. Taking time each day for mindfulness can reduce anxiety and create a sense of calm, making it easier to navigate the emotional ups and downs that the holidays may bring. Integrating these practices into daily routines can foster resilience and promote emotional well-being throughout the season.

Self-care routines become especially important during the busy holiday schedule. It is easy to become so caught up in the hustle and bustle that personal needs are placed on the back burner. Recognizing the importance of self-care means understanding that it is not a luxury but a necessity for emotional health. Setting aside time for activities that bring joy, such as reading, taking walks in nature, or engaging in creative pursuits, can provide a much-needed respite from the demands of the holidays. Making a conscious effort to prioritize self-care can help mitigate the symptoms of SAD and enhance overall well-being.

Creating a stress-free holiday calendar can also play a significant role in managing the emotional challenges associated with the season. By planning ahead and allowing for flexibility, individuals can reduce the sense of overwhelm that often accompanies holiday preparations. Identifying key dates and activities that matter most can help streamline efforts and minimize unnecessary stress. Incorporating time for relaxation and mindful pauses into the calendar can serve as reminders to slow down and check in with oneself. By recognizing symptoms and triggers and implementing these strategies, individuals can navigate the holiday season with greater ease and cultivate a sense of joy and peace amidst the challenges.

The Link Between Holidays and SAD

The holiday season is often depicted as a time of joy and celebration, yet for many who suffer from Seasonal Affective Disorder (SAD), this period can amplify feelings of sadness and isolation. The contrast between the expectations surrounding the holidays and the reality of experiencing SAD can be jarring. As families gather and festivities unfold, those grappling with the symptoms of SAD may find themselves feeling increasingly disconnected and overwhelmed. Understanding this link between the holidays and seasonal depression is a crucial step in managing these feelings and finding a sense of peace.

The shorter days and reduced sunlight during the winter months can have a profound effect on mood and energy levels. This seasonal change often coincides with the holidays, creating a perfect storm for those who are already vulnerable to depressive symptoms. The festive atmosphere, filled with lights and social gatherings, can serve as a painful reminder of what others seem to be experiencing. Acknowledging that these feelings are common can help in recognizing that you are not alone in your struggles during this time. This awareness can be the first step towards seeking support and implementing coping strategies.

Mindfulness techniques can play a pivotal role in managing holiday stress and SAD. Practicing mindfulness allows individuals to stay grounded in the present moment, reducing feelings of anxiety and sadness that can arise from overwhelming holiday demands. Simple practices, such as deep breathing exercises or mindful walking, can provide a much-needed respite amidst the chaos of holiday planning and family gatherings. By integrating mindfulness into your daily routine, you can create moments of calm that counterbalance the stress often associated with this season.

Family dynamics can also intensify stress during the holidays, particularly for those dealing with SAD. The pressure to participate in gatherings or maintain traditions can feel burdensome, especially when mental health is compromised. Open communication with loved ones about your feelings can foster understanding and support. Setting boundaries around your participation in holiday events, or even creating new traditions that prioritize your well-being, can help mitigate stress. It is essential to remember that self-care is not selfish; it is a necessary component of navigating this challenging time.

Creating a stress-free holiday calendar is another effective strategy for managing SAD during the holidays. Prioritizing activities that bring joy and fulfillment while allowing for downtime can help maintain balance. Incorporating self-care routines into your schedule, such as engaging in hobbies, spending time in nature, or simply resting, can provide a buffer against the emotional demands of the season. By intentionally designing your holiday experience around what you truly value, you can cultivate an environment that nurtures your mental health and fosters a sense of light, even in the darkest days of winter.

2

Managing Holiday
Stress

Common Sources of Holiday Stress

The holiday season, often portrayed as a time
of joy and togetherness, can paradoxically become
a significant source of stress, especially for those
struggling with Seasonal Affective Disorder
(SAD). The expectations surrounding the holidays
can feel overwhelming. From the pressure to create
the perfect celebration to the need to maintain a
cheerful demeanor, individuals may find themselves grappling with feelings of inadequacy and
anxiety. This can lead to a cycle of stress that exac-
erbates symptoms of depression, making it crucial

to recognize and address these common sources of holiday stress.

Family dynamics often play a pivotal role in holiday stress. Gatherings that should foster connection can sometimes bring to the surface unresolved conflicts or differences in expectations among family members. The pressure to navigate these complex relationships can be particularly challenging for those who already feel emotionally vulnerable. It's important to acknowledge these dynamics and consider strategies for maintaining boundaries and fostering open communication, which can help alleviate tensions and promote a more peaceful holiday experience.

Financial strain is another significant contributor to holiday stress. The societal pressure to give gifts, host elaborate gatherings, and participate in festive activities can lead to overspending and financial anxiety. For those managing SAD, this added burden can feel particularly heavy, as it may lead to feelings of shame or inadequacy. Recognizing that it is possible to celebrate the holidays in meaningful, budget-friendly ways can help shift the focus from materialism to connection and gratitude, allowing for a more fulfilling experience.

Time management also presents a challenge during the holiday season. The busy schedules filled with social obligations, shopping, and preparation can leave little room for self-care and relaxation. For individuals experiencing SAD, neglecting self-care routines can exacerbate feelings of sadness and overwhelm. By prioritizing mindfulness techniques and carving out time for personal well-being, individuals can create a healthier balance during the holidays, enabling them to engage in festivities without sacrificing their mental health.

Lastly, the societal narrative surrounding the holidays often emphasizes an idealized vision of happiness and togetherness, which can intensify feelings of loneliness for those dealing with SAD. The contrast between one's lived experience and these expectations can lead to a profound sense of isolation. It's essential to remember that it is okay to feel differently and to seek support during this time. By cultivating a stress-free holiday calendar that aligns with personal values and needs, individuals can reclaim their holiday experience and find moments of joy amidst the challenges.

Strategies for Reducing Holiday Anxiety

The holiday season, while often seen as a time of joy and celebration, can also bring about significant anxiety, particularly for those managing Seasonal Affective Disorder. It's essential to recognize this anxiety and employ strategies that can help mitigate its effects. One effective approach is to practice mindfulness techniques. Mindfulness encourages individuals to focus on the present moment, reducing the tendency to ruminate on past disappointments or future worries. Simple practices such as deep breathing, meditation, or even mindful walking can ground you, making the overwhelming chaos of the holidays feel more manageable.

Planning is another key strategy for reducing holiday anxiety. Creating a stress-free holiday calendar allows you to visualize your commitments and prioritize what truly matters. By setting aside time for essential activities and leaving room for spontaneity, you can alleviate the pressure of last-minute tasks. It's important to communicate your plans with family members to ensure everyone is on the same page, which can help prevent misunderstandings that often lead to increased stress. Remember, it's perfectly acceptable to say no to additional obligations that don't align with your well-being.

Family dynamics can also play a significant role in holiday stress. Open communication with family members about your feelings and needs can foster a more supportive environment. Consider having a family meeting to discuss expectations, set boundaries, and share coping strategies. Emphasizing understanding and empathy within family interactions can reduce tension and create a more harmonious atmosphere. This approach not only helps you manage your anxiety but also encourages your loved ones to be more compassionate and supportive.

Self-care is crucial during the hectic holiday season. Carving out time for yourself, even amidst busy schedules, can provide the relief you need. Whether it's indulging in a favorite hobby, reading a book, or simply enjoying a quiet cup of tea, prioritizing self-care can recharge your emotional batteries. Establishing a routine that includes regular exercise, nutritious meals, and adequate sleep can also bolster your resilience against stress and anxiety. Remember, self-care isn't selfish; it's a necessary component of maintaining your mental health.

Finally, it's vital to embrace flexibility during the holidays. Things may not go as planned, and that's okay. Allowing room for improvisation can create space for unexpected joy and connection. If something doesn't work out, try to shift your perspective and see it as an opportunity to create new traditions or memories. By practicing kindness toward yourself and others, you can navigate the holiday season with greater ease, transforming a time often marked by stress into one filled with light and connection.

Setting Realistic Expectations

Setting realistic expectations during the holiday season is crucial for individuals dealing with Seasonal Affective Disorder (SAD) and related stress. The holidays often come with a flurry of societal pressures—perfect decorations, idyllic family gatherings, and the expectation of joy and cheer. For those struggling with SAD, these ideals can feel out of reach, leading to heightened feelings of inadequacy and despair. Acknowledging that it's okay for things to be less than perfect can provide a significant relief, allowing space for a more manageable and enjoyable holiday experience.

Start by reflecting on what the holidays truly mean to you. Instead of adhering to traditional expectations, consider what brings you genuine joy and comfort. This might involve scaling back on social commitments or redefining how you celebrate. For instance, if the thought of hosting a large gathering feels overwhelming, perhaps a small, intimate dinner with close friends or family would be more fulfilling. Embracing a personalized approach can lessen the pressure and allow for moments that resonate with your individual needs and feelings.

It's also important to communicate openly with loved ones about your needs and limitations.

Family dynamics can be particularly stressful during this season, and misunderstandings can arise when expectations are not clearly expressed. By sharing your feelings and setting boundaries, you can foster a supportive environment where everyone's emotional well-being is considered. This might mean opting out of certain traditions or delegating responsibilities, which can create a more inclusive atmosphere where everyone feels comfortable.

Incorporating mindfulness techniques can further assist in managing expectations. Engaging in practices such as meditation, deep breathing, or even taking a few moments for quiet reflection can help ground you amidst the holiday chaos. These techniques allow you to reconnect with your emotional state and reassess what is truly important during this time. By focusing on the present, you can alleviate anxiety about future gatherings or potential disappointments, reminding yourself that it's okay to take things one step at a time.

Finally, establish a self-care routine that fits within your holiday schedule. This could include setting aside time for enjoyable activities, whether it's reading a book, taking a walk, or even enjoying a warm bath. Prioritizing self-care is essential, especially when managing SAD, as it empowers you to recharge and approach the holidays with a clearer mindset. By creating a stress-free holiday calendar that includes time for both obligations and personal care, you can find balance and cultivate an atmosphere of peace rather than pressure.

3

Mindfulness Techniques for Holiday Relaxation

Introduction to Mindfulness

Mindfulness is a powerful tool that can help those suffering from Seasonal Affective Disorder (SAD) navigate the challenges of the holiday season. At its core, mindfulness involves being present in the moment, allowing individuals to observe their thoughts and feelings without judgment. This practice can be particularly beneficial during the holidays, a time often filled with heightened emotions, stress, and expectations. By cultivating mindfulness, individuals can create a sense of calm and clarity amid the chaos that the holiday season can bring.

The holidays are frequently associated with joy and celebration, but for many, they can also trigger feelings of sadness, anxiety, and overwhelm. Mindfulness offers a way to counteract these negative emotions. By focusing on the present moment, individuals can develop a greater awareness of their thoughts and feelings, which can help them respond to stress rather than react impulsively. This shift in perspective can alleviate the burden of holiday pressures and allow for a more meaningful engagement with family and friends.

Incorporating mindfulness techniques into holiday routines can enhance relaxation and reduce stress. Simple practices, such as mindful breathing or short meditation sessions, can be woven into daily activities, making them easily accessible even amidst busy schedules. For instance, taking a few minutes to breathe deeply before stepping into a family gathering or focusing on the sensations of preparing a holiday meal can ground individuals in the present, fostering a sense of peace. These techniques not only promote relaxation but also encourage a deeper connection to the experiences of the season.

Family dynamics can often add layers of stress during the holidays. Mindfulness can serve as a bridge to better communication and understanding among family members. By practicing active listening and being fully present during conversations, individuals can navigate potential conflicts with greater ease. This approach fosters compassion and patience, allowing for genuine connections to flourish. Embracing mindfulness in family interactions can transform challenging moments into opportunities for growth and connection.

Ultimately, creating a stress-free holiday calendar that incorporates mindfulness practices can significantly enhance the holiday experience for those managing SAD. Prioritizing self-care and mindful moments amidst the busyness of the season can lead to a more fulfilling and balanced holiday. By intentionally scheduling time for reflection, relaxation, and connection, individuals can find light during what may feel like a dark season. Embracing mindfulness not only supports mental health but also enriches the holiday experience, allowing individuals to celebrate with authenticity and joy.

Breathing Exercises for Calmness

Breathing exercises serve as a powerful tool for fostering calmness, especially during the bustling holiday season. For individuals grappling with Seasonal Affective Disorder (SAD), the stress of holiday expectations can amplify feelings of sadness and anxiety. Incorporating simple yet effective breathing techniques into your daily routine can help create a refuge of tranquility amidst the chaos. By focusing on your breath, you can anchor yourself in the present moment, allowing you to observe your thoughts and feelings without becoming overwhelmed.

One of the most accessible breathing exercises is the 4-7-8 technique. To practice this, find a comfortable position, either sitting or lying down. Inhale deeply through your nose for a count of four, allowing your abdomen to expand. Hold your breath for a count of seven, and then exhale slowly through your mouth for a count of eight. Repeat this cycle four to five times. This exercise not only calms the mind but also helps reduce stress hormones in the body, promoting a sense of peace that can be particularly beneficial during holiday gatherings or family interactions.

Another effective method is diaphragmatic breathing, which encourages full oxygen exchange and activates the body's relaxation response. To practice, place one hand on your chest and the other on your abdomen. Inhale deeply through your nose, ensuring that your stomach rises while your chest remains relatively still. Exhale slowly and fully through your mouth. This technique not only combats feelings of anxiety but also enhances your overall mood, making it easier to engage positively with loved ones during the often-challenging holiday season.

Incorporating breath awareness into mindful moments throughout your day can create a lasting impact on your mental state. Consider setting aside a few minutes each morning to breathe consciously. As you prepare for the day's activities, take this time to reconnect with your breath, allowing it to serve as a reminder of your intention to approach the holidays with calmness and clarity. This practice can be particularly beneficial when navigating family dynamics, as it helps cultivate patience and understanding, essential qualities when tensions may arise.

Lastly, remember that self-care is an ongoing journey, especially during the holidays. Create a personalized holiday calendar that includes dedicated time for breathing exercises, alongside other self-care routines. Whether it's a quiet morning ritual, an afternoon break, or a moment of pause during a busy family gathering, prioritizing these moments can significantly enhance your ability to manage stress and sadness. By embracing the power of your breath, you can find light even in the most challenging holiday seasons, fostering a sense of peace that radiates throughout your days.

Guided Meditations for the Holidays

Guided meditations can serve as a powerful tool for those navigating the complexities of the holiday season, especially for individuals dealing with Seasonal Affective Disorder (SAD). The holidays can often amplify feelings of sadness and anxiety, making it crucial to incorporate mindfulness practices that foster a sense of peace and clarity. These meditations provide a structured way to step back from the hustle and bustle, enabling you to reconnect with your inner self and cultivate a serene mindset amidst the chaos.

As you embark on your journey through the holidays, consider setting aside time for daily guided meditations. These can range from just a few minutes to longer sessions, depending on your schedule. By dedicating even a small portion of your day to meditation, you create a sanctuary for yourself—a space to breathe deeply, reflect, and release the tensions that may arise from family dynamics or holiday obligations. Focus on your breath and allow the soothing guidance to help you center your thoughts and emotions, letting go of the weight of expectations.

Incorporating guided meditations into your self-care routine can also enhance your ability to manage stress effectively. During times of family gatherings or social events, the pressure to maintain a cheerful demeanor can be overwhelming. Practicing mindfulness before these interactions can help you prepare mentally and emotionally. Visualizing positive outcomes or simply grounding yourself in the present moment can create a buffer against stressors, allowing you to engage with loved ones more authentically and with greater ease.

Creating a stress-free holiday calendar often requires intentional planning. Guided meditations can play a role in this process by providing clarity on what truly matters to you during the season. As you meditate, contemplate your priorities and the activities that bring you joy, rather than obligation. This reflection can help you delineate between what is essential and what might be excessive, leading to a more balanced and fulfilling holiday experience. By aligning your calendar with your values, you foster an environment that supports your mental well-being.

Ultimately, the goal of integrating guided meditations into your holiday practices is to cultivate resilience and a deeper sense of self-compassion. The holiday season presents unique challenges, but by actively engaging in mindfulness, you can reclaim your peace and joy. Embrace the power of these guided sessions as a gentle reminder that your feelings are valid and that it is possible to navigate this time with grace. Allow yourself the gift of presence, both for yourself and those around you, as you find light in the midst of the season's demands.

Practicing Gratitude

Practicing gratitude is an essential tool for those navigating the challenges of Seasonal Affective Disorder (SAD) and the stress that often accompanies the holiday season. In moments when darkness feels overwhelming, intentionally focusing on what we appreciate in our lives can illuminate paths toward emotional resilience. Gratitude shifts our perspective, allowing us to recognize the small joys that exist even amidst the heavier feelings of the season. This shift in focus is not just a fleeting exercise but a practice that can be woven into the fabric of our daily lives, fostering a more positive mindset.

Begin this practice by setting aside a few moments each day to reflect on what you are grateful for—no matter how small. It could be the warmth of a cup of tea, a favorite song on the radio, or the laughter of loved ones. Keeping a gratitude journal can be particularly beneficial; writing down these thoughts provides a tangible reminder of positivity when darker thoughts might surface. During the holiday season, try to make it a family activity. Sharing gratitude with loved ones can strengthen bonds and create a supportive environment, making the season feel less isolating.

Mindfulness techniques can enhance your gratitude practice, making it deeper and more resonant. When you engage in mindfulness, you become more aware of the present moment, which allows you to fully appreciate the good things in your life as they happen. Try to incorporate mindfulness into your gratitude practice by taking a few moments to sit quietly and reflect. Breathe deeply, letting go of distractions, and focus on the feelings of gratitude in your heart. This simple act can create a sense of calm that counteracts holiday stress and deepens your connection to the season's positive aspects.

Family dynamics during the holidays can bring both joy and tension. Practicing gratitude can serve as a bridge to smoother interactions with relatives. When faced with challenging situations, take a moment to remember what you appreciate about your family. This could be shared traditions, memories, or even the quirks that make each person unique. By approaching family gatherings with a mindset of gratitude, you can foster a more harmonious environment, allowing you to enjoy the company of loved ones more fully, despite the stresses that may arise.

Finally, integrating gratitude into your self-care routine during the busy holiday season can help you maintain balance. Amidst the hustle and bustle, it is vital to carve out time for yourself. This can include quiet reflection, spending time in nature, or simply enjoying a moment of stillness. Practicing gratitude as part of your self-care not only nurtures your spirit but also serves as a reminder to appreciate the progress you make in managing your well-being. By creating a stress-free holiday calendar that includes time for gratitude, mindfulness, and self-care, you can navigate the season with a renewed sense of hope and light.

4

Family Dynamics and Stress Management Over the Hol

Navigating Family Expectations

Navigating family expectations during the holiday season can be particularly challenging for those suffering from Seasonal Affective Disorder (SAD). The pressure to uphold traditions, meet familial obligations, and maintain a cheerful demeanor can intensify feelings of sadness and overwhelm. Understanding that it's okay to feel this way is the first step toward managing these expectations. Acknowledging your feelings can help you create a

more realistic approach to the holidays, allowing
you to prioritize your mental health and well-being.

Communication is key when it comes to family
dynamics. Openly discussing your feelings with
family members can help alleviate some of the
pressure you may feel. Sharing your experience
with SAD can foster understanding and compassion among your loved ones. They may not fully
grasp what you're going through, but expressing
your needs can lead to support and accommoda-
tions that make holiday gatherings more manageable. Consider setting aside time to have these
conversations before the holiday rush begins, giving your family the opportunity to adjust their expectations accordingly.

Mindfulness techniques can serve as powerful
tools for navigating family expectations. Practicing
mindfulness can help you stay present and
grounded amidst the chaos of holiday preparations. Simple exercises, such as deep breathing or
guided meditation, can create moments of calm
that allow you to reconnect with your inner self.
Incorporating these practices into your daily rou-

tine can enhance your resilience, making it easier to handle family interactions that may otherwise feel overwhelming. By prioritizing mindfulness, you can cultivate a sense of peace that carries you through the season.

Establishing self-care routines is vital during the holidays, especially for those juggling family obligations and personal struggles with SAD. Carving out time for activities that nourish your spirit can significantly impact your mental health. Whether it's indulging in a favorite book, taking a quiet walk, or practicing a creative hobby, these moments of self-care can provide a much-needed respite from holiday stressors. Schedule these activities into your calendar to ensure they don't get lost in the busyness of the season, reinforcing the importance of your well-being.

Creating a stress-free holiday calendar can help manage expectations and reduce anxiety. Plan ahead by outlining family gatherings, shopping trips, and self-care moments in a way that feels balanced. Include time for rest and recovery to prevent burnout. Being intentional about your schedule allows you to make choices that align with your needs and energy levels. Remember, it's okay to say no to certain events or obligations if they don't serve your mental health. By prioritizing what truly matters to you, you can navigate family expectations with greater ease and find more joy in the holiday season.

Communicating Needs and Boundaries

Communicating needs and boundaries is an essential skill for anyone navigating the complexities of the holiday season, especially for those experiencing Seasonal Affective Disorder (SAD). The holidays can evoke a mix of emotions, from joy to anxiety, and it is vital to articulate your feelings and requirements to those around you. By being open about your emotional state and the challenges you face, you create an environment that encourages understanding and support. This communication helps to alleviate some of the pressures that can lead to stress and overwhelm during this time.

Establishing clear boundaries is equally important. During the holidays, it may be tempting to overcommit to various events and gatherings, driven by a desire to maintain traditions or meet family expectations. However, recognizing your limits and expressing them to others is crucial for your mental well-being. Whether it's declining an invitation to a large family gathering or setting aside quiet time for yourself, communicating these boundaries can prevent feelings of resentment and burnout. It is a healthy practice that prioritizes your emotional needs, allowing for a more enjoyable holiday experience.

Incorporating mindfulness techniques into your communication can further enhance your ability to express needs and boundaries. Mindfulness encourages you to remain present in your interactions, ensuring that your words reflect your true feelings rather than reactions to external pressures. Practicing mindfulness can help you approach conversations with a sense of calm, making it easier to articulate what you need without feeling overwhelmed. This approach not only improves your communication but also models healthy behavior for others, encouraging them to be mindful in their own interactions with you.

Family dynamics can often complicate the process of communicating needs and boundaries. Each family member may have differing expectations and traditions, which can lead to misunderstandings or conflicts. It's essential to approach these conversations with empathy and patience, acknowledging that everyone is navigating their own challenges. By fostering an open dialogue, you create a space where family members can express their feelings, leading to a more harmonious atmosphere. This understanding can help shift the focus from obligation to genuine connection, allowing for a more meaningful holiday experience.

Lastly, developing a self-care routine that aligns with your holiday schedule is vital for maintaining your well-being. As you communicate your needs, integrate self-care practices that resonate with you, such as journaling, meditation, or quiet reflection. Share these practices with your loved ones, inviting them to understand how they can support you. By doing so, you not only prioritize your mental health but also encourage a culture of care and mindfulness within your family and social circles. This holistic approach to communication empowers you to celebrate the holidays in a way that honors both your needs and the connections you cherish.

Conflict Resolution Strategies

Conflict resolution strategies are essential tools for navigating the often tumultuous waters of holiday gatherings, especially for those experiencing seasonal affective disorder (SAD). The holiday season can amplify feelings of stress and anxiety, particularly when family dynamics come into play. Understanding how to address and manage conflicts can lead to a more peaceful and enjoyable experience, allowing you to focus on the joy of the season rather than the tensions that may arise.

One effective strategy is to practice active listening. During family discussions, it's vital to truly hear what others are saying rather than simply waiting for your turn to speak. This not only helps in understanding different perspectives but also fosters a sense of empathy. When you acknowledge others' feelings and viewpoints, it can reduce defensiveness and pave the way for more constructive conversations. Incorporating mindfulness techniques, such as taking deep breaths or pausing before responding, can enhance your ability to listen and engage thoughtfully.

Setting clear boundaries is another crucial aspect of conflict resolution. Before holiday gatherings, take some time to reflect on your limits regarding topics of discussion or behaviors that might trigger stress. Communicate these boundaries calmly and assertively to your family members. By doing so, you not only protect your mental well-being but also set the tone for a more respectful and understanding environment. It's important to remember that boundaries are not walls; they are guidelines that help everyone feel more comfortable and respected.

In moments of conflict, it is beneficial to focus on solutions rather than problems. When disagreements arise, shift the conversation towards finding common ground or compromises that can satisfy all parties involved. This approach encourages collaboration and minimizes feelings of hostility. Practicing gratitude during these discussions can also be powerful, as it reminds everyone involved of the underlying love and connection that the holiday season embodies. A simple acknowledgment of what you appreciate about one another can diffuse tension and foster a spirit of cooperation.

Finally, self-care should remain a priority throughout the holiday season. When conflicts arise, it can be easy to neglect your own needs in favor of family obligations. However, managing your mental health during this time is crucial, especially for those susceptible to SAD. Create a self-care routine that includes activities that bring you joy and relaxation, whether it's a quiet walk, journaling, or spending time with supportive friends. By taking care of yourself, you enhance your ability to handle conflicts gracefully and maintain a sense of calm amidst the holiday chaos. Remember, the goal is not to eliminate conflict altogether but to navigate it with grace and understanding, allowing the light of the season to shine through.

5

Self-Care Routines for Busy Holiday Schedules

Prioritizing Self-Care

Prioritizing self-care during the holiday season is essential, especially for those experiencing Seasonal Affective Disorder (SAD). The pressure to maintain a festive atmosphere can often exacerbate feelings of sadness and anxiety. Acknowledging the need for self-care is the first step towards managing these emotions. It is crucial to create space for yourself amidst the chaos, allowing for moments of reflection and rejuvenation. By prioritizing your well-being, you can navigate the holiday season with greater ease and resilience.

One effective way to prioritize self-care is to establish a daily routine that incorporates mindfulness techniques. Simple practices such as deep breathing, meditation, or gentle yoga can help ground you in the present moment, reducing stress and promoting emotional balance. Even a few minutes each day dedicated to these activities can make a significant difference in your overall mood. Consider setting aside time in the morning or evening to engage in these practices, creating a sanctuary of calm in your busy holiday schedule.

Family dynamics can add another layer of complexity to the holiday season. It is essential to establish boundaries and communicate your needs to loved ones. Discussing your feelings openly can foster understanding and support, allowing family members to be more considerate of your emotional state. Remember, it is okay to decline invitations or request a quieter, more intimate gathering if that aligns better with your self-care needs. Prioritizing your mental health is not only beneficial for you but can also create a more harmonious atmosphere for everyone involved.

Creating a stress-free holiday calendar is another effective strategy for prioritizing self-care. Mapping out your commitments and responsibilities can help you visualize your time and energy. Be intentional about scheduling downtime and activities that bring you joy. This might include leisurely walks, reading, or engaging in a favorite hobby. By planning moments of relaxation alongside your holiday tasks, you ensure that self-care remains a priority rather than an afterthought in the hustle and bustle of the season.

Ultimately, prioritizing self-care during the holidays is about recognizing your own needs and taking proactive steps to meet them. As you navigate feelings of sadness and stress, remember that it is not selfish to take time for yourself; it is necessary. By incorporating mindfulness, setting boundaries, creating a balanced calendar, and allowing yourself moments of joy, you can find light amidst the seasonal shadows. Embrace the journey of self-care, and let it guide you towards a more fulfilling and peaceful holiday experience.

Quick and Effective Self-Care Practices

Quick and effective self-care practices are essential for those experiencing Seasonal Affective Disorder (SAD), especially during the often overwhelming holiday season. Acknowledging the unique challenges that come with this time of year, it's crucial to incorporate simple yet powerful self-care techniques into your daily routine. These practices can help alleviate stress, promote a sense of well-being, and offer moments of tranquility amidst the hustle and bustle.

One of the most effective self-care practices is to establish a daily mindfulness routine. Mindfulness can take many forms, such as meditation, deep breathing exercises, or even a few moments of quiet reflection. Setting aside just ten minutes each day to center yourself can significantly improve your mood and reduce feelings of anxiety. Find a quiet space, close your eyes, and focus on your breath. Allow any thoughts or worries to drift away like clouds in the sky. This small investment of time can create a ripple effect, helping you navigate holiday stress with greater ease.

Incorporating physical activity into your daily life is another vital self-care practice. During the holidays, it can be tempting to withdraw and become sedentary, yet movement is a powerful tool for combating feelings of sadness and stress. Whether it's a brisk walk in the fresh air, a gentle yoga session, or dancing in your living room, find an activity that brings you joy and make it a regular part of your routine. Aim for at least 30 minutes each day, but remember that every little bit counts. Engaging in physical activity can release endorphins, improve your mood, and provide a sense of accomplishment.

Creating a stress-free holiday calendar can also serve as an effective self-care strategy. The holidays can feel chaotic, with numerous commitments pulling you in different directions. To alleviate this pressure, take some time to map out your schedule. Prioritize activities that bring you joy and fulfillment while also allowing space for relaxation. Set boundaries by saying no to events that may drain your energy or exacerbate your feelings of stress. By intentionally crafting your holiday calendar, you can create an environment that supports your mental health and allows you to savor the season.

Lastly, don't underestimate the power of connection, even if it's virtual or limited. Reach out to friends or family members who understand what you're going through. Sharing your thoughts and feelings can provide immense relief and help combat feelings of isolation associated with SAD. Consider scheduling regular check-ins, whether through phone calls, video chats, or even text messages. These connections can provide a support system that reminds you you're not alone in your experiences. By embracing these quick and effective self-care practices, you can navigate the holiday season with resilience and grace, nurturing both your mind and spirit.

Integrating Self-Care into Holiday Activities

Integrating self-care into holiday activities is essential for those who experience seasonal affective disorder (SAD) and the holiday stress that often accompanies this time of year. The holidays can be a whirlwind of commitments, expectations, and emotional triggers. By prioritizing self-care, you can create a more balanced and fulfilling holiday experience. Start by acknowledging your own needs and recognizing that it's okay to step back from the hustle and bustle. This can set a more positive tone for your holiday season.

One effective way to incorporate self-care is by creating a personalized holiday calendar. Instead of filling your schedule with obligatory events and gatherings, take time to map out activities that truly resonate with you. Include moments of solitude, relaxation, and joy, such as quiet evenings with a favorite book, leisurely walks in nature, or even short meditation sessions. By intentionally scheduling these self-care moments, you are honoring your well-being and ensuring that you have the energy to engage meaningfully in holiday traditions.

Mindfulness techniques can serve as powerful tools during this busy season. Simple practices like deep breathing, progressive muscle relaxation, or guided visualization can ground you amidst the chaos. Incorporate these techniques into your holiday routine, whether it's during family gatherings or while preparing meals. For example, taking a few moments to breathe deeply before entering a crowded room can help reduce anxiety and center your thoughts. The goal is to cultivate a sense of presence, allowing you to savor the joyful moments instead of feeling overwhelmed by them.

Family dynamics can also contribute significantly to holiday stress. It's important to communicate your self-care needs clearly with loved ones. Share your intentions for the season, whether that means opting out of certain events or suggesting alternative plans that support your mental health. Encourage open dialogues about everyone's needs and feelings, fostering a more understanding and supportive atmosphere. By actively engaging in these conversations, you create an environment where self-care is not only accepted but encouraged among family members.

Ultimately, the key to integrating self-care into holiday activities lies in balance and intention. Allow yourself the grace to say no when necessary and to prioritize your well-being. Embrace the joy of the season while also recognizing the importance of your mental health. Remember that taking care of yourself is not a selfish act; it is a vital part of being able to connect authentically with others. By weaving self-care into your holiday fabric, you can navigate the season with greater ease, finding light even in the darker months.

6

Creating a Stress-Free Holiday Calendar

Planning Ahead: The Importance of Scheduling

Planning ahead is crucial for anyone seeking to manage the unique stresses that accompany the holiday season, especially for those dealing with Seasonal Affective Disorder (SAD). The holidays, while often filled with joy and celebration, can also amplify feelings of sadness and anxiety. By establishing a clear schedule, you can create a sense of control over your environment, allowing you to navigate the emotional ups and downs that often arise during this time. Scheduling can serve as a powerful tool to help you maintain balance and prioritize self-care.

When you take the time to plan your holiday activities, you reduce the likelihood of last-minute stressors that can trigger feelings of overwhelm. Create a calendar that outlines your commitments, from family gatherings to personal time for relaxation. This proactive approach allows you to see your obligations clearly, enabling you to allocate time for activities that bring you joy and peace. While it may be tempting to fill every moment with social engagements, remember that carving out time for yourself is just as important, if not more so, for your mental well-being.

Incorporating mindfulness techniques into your planning can further enhance your holiday experience. Schedule brief moments throughout your day for mindfulness practices, such as deep breathing or meditation. These practices can help ground you during chaotic moments and serve as a reminder to remain present, even when holiday pressures begin to accumulate. By intentionally including mindfulness in your schedule, you create spaces for reflection and calm amid the hustle and bustle, making it easier to cope with feelings of sadness that may arise.

Family dynamics can be a source of tension during the holidays, particularly when combined with the emotional challenges of SAD. Establishing a schedule can help manage these dynamics by setting boundaries around family interactions. Communicate your needs to loved ones early on, allowing them to understand the importance of respecting your limits. This can create a more supportive atmosphere, where everyone is aware of your emotional state and can contribute to a more harmonious holiday experience.

Ultimately, the key to a successful holiday season lies in the balance between scheduling and flexibility. Life can be unpredictable, and it's important to allow yourself the grace to adapt when things don't go as planned. By maintaining an awareness of your mental health needs while also embracing the spontaneity that holidays can bring, you can create a stress-free holiday calendar that nurtures your well-being. Planning ahead empowers you to celebrate the season in a way that honors both your traditions and your health, allowing you to find light even in the darkest of times.

Balancing Activities and Downtime

Finding a balance between activities and downtime during the holiday season can be particularly challenging for those coping with Seasonal Affective Disorder (SAD). The festive period often comes with a whirlwind of gatherings, shopping, and other obligations that can quickly overwhelm even the most resilient individuals. For those suffering from SAD, the bright lights and joyous sounds can sometimes amplify feelings of sadness and fatigue. It is essential to recognize that not every moment needs to be filled with activity. Carving out intentional spaces for rest and reflection is vital to managing both holiday stress and the symptoms of SAD.

Mindfulness techniques can play a crucial role in achieving this balance. Practicing mindfulness allows you to remain present and aware, helping you to differentiate between the moments that require your full engagement and those that call for a pause. Simple techniques such as deep breathing, meditation, or even a brief moment of gratitude can help ground you. When you find yourself feeling overwhelmed by a busy schedule, taking a few minutes to center yourself can create a clear distinction between necessary activities and the downtime you desperately need. This shift in focus can foster a sense of calm and clarity amidst the chaos.

Family dynamics often add another layer of complexity to the holiday season. Family gatherings can be filled with joy, but they can also trigger stress, especially for those dealing with mental health challenges. It's crucial to communicate your needs with family members and set boundaries that allow for both participation in family events and time for self-care. This could mean stepping away for a quiet moment during a loud gathering or declining an invitation when you feel your energy waning. By openly discussing your feelings and intentions, you not only advocate for your own well-being but also model healthy communication for your loved ones.

Creating a stress-free holiday calendar is an effective strategy to manage both activities and downtime. By planning out your schedule in advance, you can allocate specific times for social events while ensuring that you also reserve blocks of time for rest. Consider incorporating rituals that promote relaxation, such as cozy evenings at home with a good book or quiet walks in nature. These moments of tranquility can be sprinkled throughout your calendar, providing you with essential breaks to recharge. A well-balanced calendar can serve as a protective buffer against the overwhelming nature of the holidays.

Ultimately, the key to balancing activities and downtime lies in self-awareness and self-compassion. Acknowledge that it's okay to feel less than festive, and allow yourself the grace to step back when needed. Prioritize what truly matters to you during this season, focusing on meaningful connections rather than obligations. By honoring your feelings and needs, you can create a holiday experience that not only minimizes stress but also fosters a sense of peace and joy, even in the face of SAD.

Flexibility and Adaptability in Planning

Flexibility and adaptability are essential components in the planning process, especially for those grappling with Seasonal Affective Disorder (SAD) during the holidays. The festive season often brings a mix of expectations and obligations that can feel overwhelming, particularly for those already dealing with the emotional weight of SAD. By embracing a flexible mindset, you can navigate the complexities of holiday planning with greater ease. This approach allows you to respond to your feelings and circumstances rather than rigidly adhering to a predetermined agenda that may exacerbate stress.

When planning holiday activities, consider incorporating a variety of options that suit your mood and energy levels. Some days, you might feel up to participating in family gatherings, while other days may call for quieter, more introspective moments. By allowing yourself the freedom to choose based on how you feel, you can create a more balanced experience. This flexibility not only reduces stress but also fosters an environment where self-care becomes a priority, enabling you to engage in activities that genuinely uplift your spirit.

Mindfulness techniques can play a crucial role in helping you remain adaptable during this busy season. Practicing mindfulness encourages you to stay present and focused on the moment, which can be particularly beneficial when faced with unexpected changes in plans or family dynamics. When you practice mindfulness, you cultivate awareness of your thoughts and emotions, allowing you to respond thoughtfully rather than react impulsively. This can help mitigate feelings of anxiety and frustration, creating space for more peaceful interactions with loved ones.

In addition to mindfulness, establishing a self-care routine tailored to your holiday schedule is an effective way to maintain balance. This routine should be flexible enough to accommodate the inevitable unpredictability of the season. Whether it's taking short breaks for deep breathing, engaging in light exercise, or dedicating time for creative expression, prioritizing self-care will help you recharge amidst the chaos. Remember, it is not only acceptable but essential to prioritize your well-being, even in the midst of holiday festivities.

Finally, creating a stress-free holiday calendar can serve as a practical tool for managing your time and commitments. While it's important to plan ahead, ensure that your calendar allows for spontaneity and change. Include buffer times between events to give yourself space to rest and recalibrate. By approaching your holiday planning with a mindset of flexibility and adaptability, you can cultivate a more enjoyable and fulfilling experience, one that honors your needs and allows you to find light even in the darker months.

7

Building a Support System

Identifying Your Support Network

Identifying your support network is a crucial step in managing the challenges that come with Seasonal Affective Disorder (SAD) and holiday stress. During this time, feelings of isolation can intensify, making it all the more important to recognize the people around you who can provide support. Your support network can consist of family members, friends, colleagues, or even community resources that understand your struggles. Acknowledging who you can turn to for help is the first step in building a system that will help you navigate the complexities of the holiday season.

Start by reflecting on your relationships. Who do you feel comfortable talking to about your feelings? Consider those who have shown empathy and understanding in the past. It may be a close friend who always listens or a family member who has supported you through difficult times. Write down these individuals and think about how they can help you. They may not have all the answers, but their presence can provide comfort and reassurance when you need it most. Even a simple conversation can alleviate some of the stress and anxiety that holidays often bring.

It's also important to recognize that your support network can extend beyond personal relationships. Community support groups, online forums, and mental health professionals can provide additional layers of understanding and connection. These resources often offer a safe space to share your experiences with others who are going through similar challenges. Finding local or online SAD support groups can help you feel less alone and provide valuable coping strategies. Engaging with these communities can empower you to take control of your mental health during the holiday season.

In addition to identifying individuals, consider how to actively engage with your support network. Plan regular check-ins with loved ones, whether in person, over the phone, or through video chats. These connections can serve as a lifeline during particularly tough days. Don't hesitate to reach out when you're feeling overwhelmed; your network likely wants to be there for you, but they may not know how unless you communicate your needs. Also, be open to sharing your feelings and experiences. Vulnerability can deepen relationships and foster a sense of shared understanding.

Lastly, remember that self-care is an integral part of your support network. As you identify the people who can help, also think about the activities and practices that uplift you. Mindfulness techniques, such as meditation or deep breathing exercises, can provide immediate relief during stressful moments. Prioritize your self-care routines, even amidst the holiday rush, to ensure you are in the best mental space possible. By recognizing and nurturing both your support network and your self-care practices, you can create a more manageable and fulfilling holiday experience, fostering resilience against the pressures of SAD and seasonal stress.

Seeking Professional Help

Seeking professional help can be a pivotal step in managing Seasonal Affective Disorder (SAD) and the stress that often accompanies the holiday season. Many individuals find themselves grappling with overwhelming emotions during this time, and it is essential to acknowledge that seeking assistance is a sign of strength, not weakness. Mental health professionals can provide support, guidance, and coping strategies tailored to your unique situation, helping you navigate the complexities of the holidays with greater ease.

When considering professional help, it is important to explore the options available to you. Therapists, psychologists, and counselors can offer different approaches, such as cognitive-behavioral therapy (CBT), which has proven effective for treating SAD. These professionals can help you identify negative thought patterns and develop healthier ways to cope with the emotional challenges that arise during the holiday season. Additionally, support groups can provide a sense of community, allowing you to share experiences with others who understand what you're going through.

Mindfulness techniques can also be integrated into your sessions with a mental health professional. Practicing mindfulness can help ground you, enabling you to stay present and manage the anxiety that often peaks during the holidays. Techniques such as guided imagery, deep breathing, and meditation can be beneficial. A therapist can help you establish a personalized mindfulness routine that fits seamlessly into your busy holiday schedule, making it easier to prioritize self-care amidst the chaos.

Family dynamics can significantly impact how we feel during the holidays. If you are dealing with challenging relationships or past traumas that resurface during this time, a professional can help you navigate these complexities. They can equip you with tools to communicate more effectively with loved ones, set healthy boundaries, and foster a more supportive environment. This can lead to a more peaceful holiday experience, allowing you to focus on what truly matters—connection and joy.

Ultimately, seeking professional help is not just about alleviating symptoms; it is about creating a sustainable framework for emotional well-being. As you work with a mental health professional, you will learn not only to cope with the immediate stressors of the holiday season but also to develop long-term strategies for managing SAD. This proactive approach ensures that you can find light even in the darkest months, empowering you to embrace the holidays with a renewed sense of hope and resilience.

Engaging in Community Activities

Engaging in community activities during the holiday season can be a powerful antidote to the feelings of isolation and sadness that often accompany Seasonal Affective Disorder (SAD). When the days grow shorter and the weather turns colder, it can be all too easy to retreat into ourselves. However, participating in community events or volunteer opportunities can provide a sense of connection and purpose that helps to alleviate these feelings. Whether it's joining a local charity drive, attending community gatherings, or participating in holiday festivities, these activities can enhance your mood and provide a welcome distraction from personal struggles.

One of the greatest benefits of community involvement is the opportunity it presents for social interaction. Engaging with others who share similar interests or values fosters a sense of belonging. This connection can be particularly important during the holidays when feelings of loneliness may intensify. By reaching out to your community, you can create new friendships and strengthen existing ones, contributing to a more supportive social network. This sense of belonging can be a vital resource in managing the symptoms of SAD, reminding you that you are not alone in your experiences.

Volunteer work, in particular, can be a fulfilling way to engage with your community while also benefiting others. Whether it's serving meals at a local shelter, participating in toy drives, or helping with holiday events, giving back can serve to shift the focus away from your own struggles. The act of helping others can ignite feelings of gratitude and joy, which can be incredibly transformative during the darker months. Moreover, volunteering can provide a structured activity that helps to fill your time and keep your mind engaged, reducing the likelihood of ruminating on negative thoughts.

Mindfulness can also play a significant role in how you approach community activities. Being present during these engagements allows you to fully appreciate the interactions and experiences as they unfold. Practicing mindfulness techniques, such as deep breathing or briefly reflecting on your feelings before participating in an event, can enhance your ability to enjoy these moments. This mindful approach can help you savor the joy of connection, fostering a deeper emotional engagement with both the activities and the people around you.

Creating a holiday calendar that incorporates community events can also be a helpful strategy in managing holiday stress. By planning ahead, you can ensure that you allocate time for both self-care and community involvement. This balanced approach allows you to prioritize your well-being while still engaging with the festive spirit of the season. Remember, it's important to listen to your own needs; if a particular event feels overwhelming, it's okay to take a step back. The goal is to find light in the season, and community activities can be a significant source of that illumination when approached thoughtfully.

8

Embracing Joy and Connection

Finding Meaning in Holiday Traditions

Finding meaning in holiday traditions can be a powerful antidote to the stress and melancholy that often accompany this season, especially for those who suffer from Seasonal Affective Disorder (SAD). As the holidays approach, it is easy to feel overwhelmed by the expectations and obligations that come with them. However, taking the time to reflect on the deeper significance of these traditions can help ground us and bring joy amidst the chaos. By focusing on what truly matters, we can transform our experience of the holidays from one of stress to one of connection and fulfillment.

Engaging in holiday traditions often serves as a reminder of our values and the people we cherish. Whether it's preparing a favorite family recipe, decorating a tree, or attending a local festival, these rituals provide a sense of continuity and belonging. For individuals experiencing SAD, these familiar practices can create moments of light and joy that counteract feelings of isolation and sadness. Embracing the nostalgia associated with these traditions can foster a sense of comfort, allowing us to reconnect with cherished memories and the warmth of family bonds.

Mindfulness techniques can enhance our experience of holiday traditions, encouraging us to be present in the moment rather than succumbing to stress. By slowing down and savoring each aspect of our rituals, we can cultivate a deeper appreciation for the season. Simple practices, such as taking a few deep breaths before engaging in a holiday task or consciously noting the textures and scents around us, can help us remain anchored in the present. This mindfulness not only alleviates anxiety but also enriches our connection to the traditions we hold dear.

Self-care becomes essential during the busy holiday season, particularly for those navigating the challenges of SAD. In this context, finding meaning in traditions can also involve setting boundaries and prioritizing our well-being. It is important to remember that it's perfectly acceptable to modify or even skip certain activities that may feel overwhelming. Instead, we can focus on what brings us joy and fulfillment. This might mean choosing to have a quiet evening at home with a favorite holiday film instead of attending a large gathering, allowing us to recharge while still honoring the spirit of the season.

Creating a stress-free holiday calendar can further facilitate the process of finding meaning in our traditions. By planning activities that resonate with our values and needs, we can approach the season with intention rather than dread. This involves identifying key traditions that uplift us and dedicating time to engage in them mindfully. Balancing these cherished practices with periods of rest and self-care will not only help manage stress but also ensure that we experience the holidays in a way that feels authentic and meaningful. In this way, the season can truly become a time of reflection, connection, and renewed hope.

Creating New Positive Experiences

Creating new positive experiences during the holiday season can be a powerful antidote to the feelings of sadness and stress that often accompany Seasonal Affective Disorder. This time of year, with its emphasis on joy and connection, can feel overwhelming, especially for those struggling with depression. However, by intentionally crafting new experiences, you can shift your focus from what feels burdensome to what can uplift your spirit. The key is to engage in activities that resonate with you and foster genuine connections, allowing you to create lasting memories that can provide comfort and joy.

One approach to cultivating positive experiences is to engage in mindfulness practices that encourage you to be present in the moment. This might mean taking a few moments each day to breathe deeply, savoring the aroma of seasonal spices, or appreciating the beauty of winter landscapes. Mindfulness can ground you, helping to reduce anxiety and elevate your mood. Consider incorporating mindful walks into your routine, where you focus on the sights and sounds of the season. This simple practice can transform a mundane task into a cherished experience, allowing you to find joy even in the ordinary.

Additionally, think about ways to involve your family in creating these new experiences. Family dynamics can be a source of stress during the holidays, but they can also be a source of warmth and connection. Plan activities that everyone can participate in, such as baking cookies together or crafting homemade decorations. These shared experiences foster a sense of teamwork and connection, reminding you of the support system that surrounds you. It is essential to communicate openly with your loved ones about your feelings, as this can lead to greater understanding and a collective effort to create a more positive holiday atmosphere.

Self-care routines play a vital role in managing holiday stress and promoting mental well-being. Prioritize time for yourself amidst the hustle and bustle by scheduling moments of rest and relaxation. This could involve reading a favorite book, enjoying a warm bath, or practicing a hobby that brings you joy. By carving out these pockets of self-care, you are not only recharging your energy but also reinforcing the idea that it is okay to take time for yourself. Remember, self-care is not selfish; it is a necessary aspect of maintaining your mental health, especially during the holiday season.

Finally, consider creating a stress-free holiday calendar that incorporates these positive experiences. Planning ahead can alleviate feelings of overwhelm and help you focus on what truly matters. List out the activities that excite you and align with your values, ensuring that you include both family-oriented events and personal self-care moments. By organizing your schedule intentionally, you can prioritize experiences that uplift you and set boundaries around those that may drain your energy. Embrace this opportunity to redefine your holiday season, allowing it to be a time of joy, connection, and healing, even amidst the challenges of SAD.

Celebrating Small Wins During the Season

Celebrating small wins during the holiday season can be a powerful antidote to the feelings of overwhelm that often accompany this time of year. For those navigating the challenges of Seasonal Affective Disorder, acknowledging even the tiniest achievements can foster a sense of accomplishment and provide a much-needed boost to mental health. Small wins can be as simple as getting out of bed on a particularly dreary morning, completing a holiday task that has been on your to-do list, or taking a moment to enjoy a favorite seasonal treat. Each of these moments, when recognized and celebrated, can help shift your focus from what might be lacking to the positive strides you are making.

Incorporating mindfulness techniques into your celebration of small wins can enhance their impact. When you take a moment to pause, breathe, and reflect on a small victory, you create space for gratitude and appreciation. Whether it's enjoying a hot cup of cocoa after wrapping gifts or taking a leisurely walk to admire holiday decorations, immersing yourself fully in these experiences allows you to savor the joy they bring. Mindfulness not only helps to anchor you in the present but also enables you to acknowledge your feelings—be they joy, relief, or even sadness—without judgment, fostering a balanced emotional landscape during the often chaotic holiday season.

Family dynamics can play a significant role in holiday stress, making it all the more crucial to celebrate small wins within this context. Recognizing that not every family gathering will be perfect can alleviate some of the pressure you may feel. Instead of fixating on the idealized holiday experience, focus on the moments that bring joy—perhaps a hearty laugh over a shared memory or a successful group activity that everyone enjoyed. By prioritizing and celebrating these moments, you create a more positive atmosphere and encourage others to do the same, allowing for a more supportive and connected family experience.

Self-care routines can sometimes feel like an impossible task during the busy holiday season, but celebrating small wins can transform your approach to self-care. Each time you carve out a few minutes for yourself—whether it's to meditate, read a book, or simply breathe deeply—you are nurturing your well-being. Acknowledging these moments as victories reminds you of the importance of self-care, encouraging you to make it a priority even when your schedule is packed. By celebrating these small acts of kindness toward yourself, you reinforce the idea that taking care of your mental health is not only acceptable but essential.

Creating a stress-free holiday calendar can also be enhanced by the practice of celebrating small wins. As you navigate your plans, be sure to include time for reflection and gratitude alongside your holiday tasks. For example, after completing a significant item on your calendar, take a moment to celebrate that achievement, whether by treating yourself to something special or simply taking a few minutes to appreciate your effort. This practice can help you maintain a sense of balance throughout the season, reminding you that each small step contributes to your overall experience of joy and fulfillment during the holidays, even in the face of challenges.

9

Reflecting and Moving Forward

Recognizing Growth and Changes

Recognizing growth and changes during the holiday season can be a profound experience for those suffering from Seasonal Affective Disorder (SAD). The festive period, often filled with joy and celebration, can also trigger feelings of sadness and stress, making it essential to acknowledge the subtle shifts in our emotions and behaviors. Understanding these changes can empower individuals to navigate their feelings more effectively and cultivate a sense of acceptance. By reflecting on personal growth, even during challenging times, one can find the strength to embrace the season with a renewed perspective.

Mindfulness plays a vital role in this recognition process. Taking moments to pause and observe our thoughts and feelings can help us identify patterns that emerge during the holidays. For instance, one might notice an increased tendency to withdraw from social gatherings or a heightened sensitivity to family dynamics. By practicing mindfulness techniques, such as deep breathing or guided meditation, individuals can create a space for self-reflection. This awareness allows for a clearer understanding of how holiday stress impacts mental well-being and opens the door to more informed decision-making.

The holidays often bring family dynamics to the forefront, which can be a double-edged sword. While reconnecting with loved ones can be uplifting, it can also stir up past grievances and increase stress levels. Recognizing growth in these interactions involves acknowledging our past responses and how they may have evolved. Perhaps one has learned to set healthier boundaries or communicate feelings more openly. Celebrating these changes, no matter how small, can foster a sense of empowerment and reduce the anxiety associated with holiday gatherings.

Self-care routines become especially crucial during this time. Busy schedules can easily overshadow the need for personal well-being, leading to feelings of burnout. Recognizing the necessity of self-care means taking intentional steps to prioritize oneself, whether through short breaks, nurturing hobbies, or engaging in physical activities. Developing a self-care plan tailored to the holiday season can help maintain emotional balance. By acknowledging the importance of these routines, individuals can combat feelings of overwhelm and create a more enjoyable holiday experience.

Creating a stress-free holiday calendar is another powerful tool for recognizing growth and changes. This approach allows individuals to visualize their commitments and make adjustments based on their emotional needs. By designating time for relaxation, family interactions, and self-care, one can cultivate a more balanced holiday experience. Recognizing the ability to create this structure is a testament to personal growth, highlighting how far one has come in managing holiday stress. Embracing these changes fosters a sense of agency, allowing individuals to approach the season not just as a time of obligation, but as an opportunity for joy, connection, and meaningful reflection.

Setting Intentions for the Next Holiday Season

As the holiday season approaches, it is not uncommon for those affected by Seasonal Affective Disorder (SAD) to experience a swell of anxiety and sadness. Setting intentions for the upcoming holiday season can serve as a powerful tool in alleviating some of the stress and emotional burden associated with this time of year. By intentionally deciding how you wish to navigate the holidays, you can create a framework that prioritizes your mental well-being, allowing you to find joy amidst the chaos.

Begin by reflecting on what the holidays mean to you. This reflection can help clarify your personal values and desires for the season. Consider what traditions bring you joy, which ones feel obligatory, and how you can modify your approach to family gatherings and celebrations. By identifying what truly matters, you can set intentions that align with your values and establish boundaries that help preserve your mental health. This might mean opting out of certain events or suggesting alternative activities that are less stressful yet still meaningful.

Mindfulness techniques can significantly enhance your experience during the holidays. Setting aside time for mindful practices, such as meditation, deep breathing, or even a simple walk in nature, can provide respite from the hustle and bustle. These practices can ground you, allowing for moments of clarity and peace amid a potentially overwhelming environment. As you move through the season, remind yourself to pause and check in with your feelings, adjusting your plans as necessary to align with your emotional state.

Creating a self-care routine tailored to the demands of the holiday season is essential. This routine should include both physical and emotional self-care practices that fit seamlessly into your busy schedule. Whether it's dedicating time for a warm bath, indulging in a favorite book, or carving out moments for quiet reflection, make sure to prioritize these actions as non-negotiable. By nurturing yourself, you equip yourself with the resilience needed to face holiday stressors and enjoy the moments that bring you joy.

Lastly, consider creating a stress-free holiday calendar that outlines your intentions, commitments, and self-care practices. This calendar can serve as a visual reminder of your priorities, helping you stay focused on what matters most. By scheduling time for both obligations and self-care, you can approach the season with a sense of purpose and control. Remember, the goal is not to achieve a picture-perfect holiday but to create a season that resonates with your true self, allowing you to find light even during the darkest days.

Continuing Mindfulness Beyond the Holidays

Continuing mindfulness beyond the holidays is essential for those grappling with Seasonal Affective Disorder (SAD) and the stress that often accompanies this time of year. The holiday season can bring moments of joy, but it can also heighten feelings of sadness and anxiety. As the decorations are taken down and the festivities come to an end, it is vital to carry forward the practices that helped cultivate a sense of peace during the holidays. Mindfulness can serve as a powerful tool to maintain a sense of balance and well-being, ensuring that you navigate the post-holiday period with intention and care.

One effective way to integrate mindfulness into your daily life is by establishing a consistent meditation practice. Spending just a few minutes each day in quiet reflection can help ground your thoughts and feelings, especially when the winter blues threaten to take hold. You might start with guided meditations designed specifically for those experiencing SAD, focusing on self-compassion and acceptance. This practice can foster a deeper connection with your emotions, allowing you to acknowledge and process them without judgment, which is crucial when the holiday glow fades.

Another aspect of mindfulness is learning to be present in everyday moments. This can be as simple as savoring your morning coffee or taking a mindful walk in nature, even if it's just around the block. Engaging your senses fully in these activities can provide a much-needed respite from racing thoughts about the past or future. By consciously bringing your awareness back to the here and now, you can cultivate a sense of gratitude and appreciation for the small joys that exist in your life, even amidst the challenges of SAD.

Family dynamics often become more pronounced during the holidays, and these interactions can leave lingering stress. Continuing mindfulness practices can help you approach family gatherings with a more compassionate mindset. By practicing empathy and understanding, you can foster healthier communication and reduce the emotional tension that may arise. Remember, it's okay to set boundaries and prioritize your mental health. Mindfulness can empower you to navigate difficult conversations with grace, ensuring that your needs are met without sacrificing your well-being.

Lastly, creating a self-care routine post-holidays is vital for maintaining the mindfulness you've cultivated. Schedule time for activities that replenish your energy and bring you joy, whether it's reading a book, engaging in a hobby, or simply resting. Design a stress-free calendar that includes these self-care moments, allowing you to look forward to them as integral parts of your week. By committing to these practices, you can not only manage the symptoms of SAD but also create a more fulfilling and balanced life beyond the holiday season.